GEOGRAPHICS

EARTHQUAKES

Georgia Amson-Bradshaw

W
FRANKLIN WATTS
LONDON·SYDNEY

Franklin Watts

First published in Great Britain in 2017 by The Watts Publishing Group

Copyright © The Watts Publishing Group 2017

Produced for Franklin Watts by
White-Thomson Publishing Ltd
www.wtpub.co.uk
01273 479982

Series Editor: Izzi Howell
Series Designer: Rocket Design (East Anglia) Ltd

Images from Shutterstock.com: Beresnev 4bl, Sentavio 4br, Stoker-13 5tl, Okuneva 5bl, RedlineVector 6c, Javid Kheyrabadi 6bl, Designua 7tr, 8t, 8bl, Clipart deSIGN 7bl, Olga Danylenko 8c, OlegD 9c, Anthro 10br, Everett Historical 11tl, Creative Mood 11br, Raftel 12c, Zern Liew 13tr, Jane Kelly 13c, Chattapat 14tr, hichako_t 14br, Creative Mood 14c, GraphicsRF 15bl, Globe Turner 16br, Lorelyn Medina 17tr, Artsholic 18tr, chombosan 19tr and c, ELENKS 20c, Denis_M 20bl, Artisticco 21tl, Raftel 22r, Kauriana 24br, Iconic Bestiary 25b, Macrovector 26tr, daulon 26c, Artwork studio BKK 26bl, Brothers Good 28cl, DEmax 28cr, HuHu 29tr, mTaira 29c, Artisticco 29b

All design elements from Shutterstock.com.
Flickr: doc searle 10bl
Wikimedia: Uwebart 17c, Felipaopsvita93 19br.
Alamy: ISSEI KATO 25c

Illustrations by Techtype: 12b, 24bl, 25t

ISBN 978 1 4451 5553 1

Printed in China

MIX
Paper from
responsible sources
FSC® C104740
FSC
www.fsc.org

Franklin Watts
An imprint of
Hachette Children's Group
Part of The Watts Publishing Group
Carmelite House
50 Victoria Embankment
London EC4Y 0DZ

An Hachette UK Company
www.hachette.co.uk
www.franklinwatts.co.uk

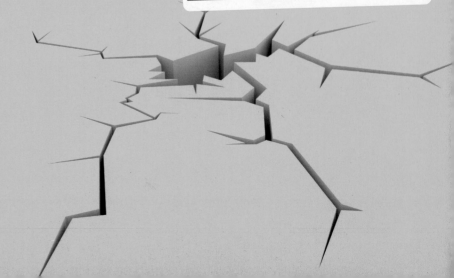

Contents

What is an Earthquake?

An earthquake is the shaking of the ground caused by movements in the Earth's crust. During a large earthquake, the ground shakes violently and buildings collapse. Cracks appear in the earth and loud noises ring through the air as structures and objects fall. For people who live in earthquake-prone areas, quakes are a constant risk.

Shockwaves

Movement in the Earth's crust (the outer layer of the Earth) causes strain to build up between large plates or blocks of rock trying to move past each other. Stored energy is released in giant shockwaves called seismic waves. These intense vibrations cause damage to buildings and streets.

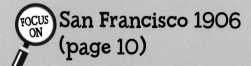 **FOCUS ON** San Francisco 1906 (page 10)

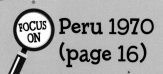 **FOCUS ON** Peru 1970 (page 16)

Regular events

Scientists estimate that there are several million earthquakes every year, however the huge majority of them go unnoticed as they are too small to be detected, or happen in remote areas.

 4

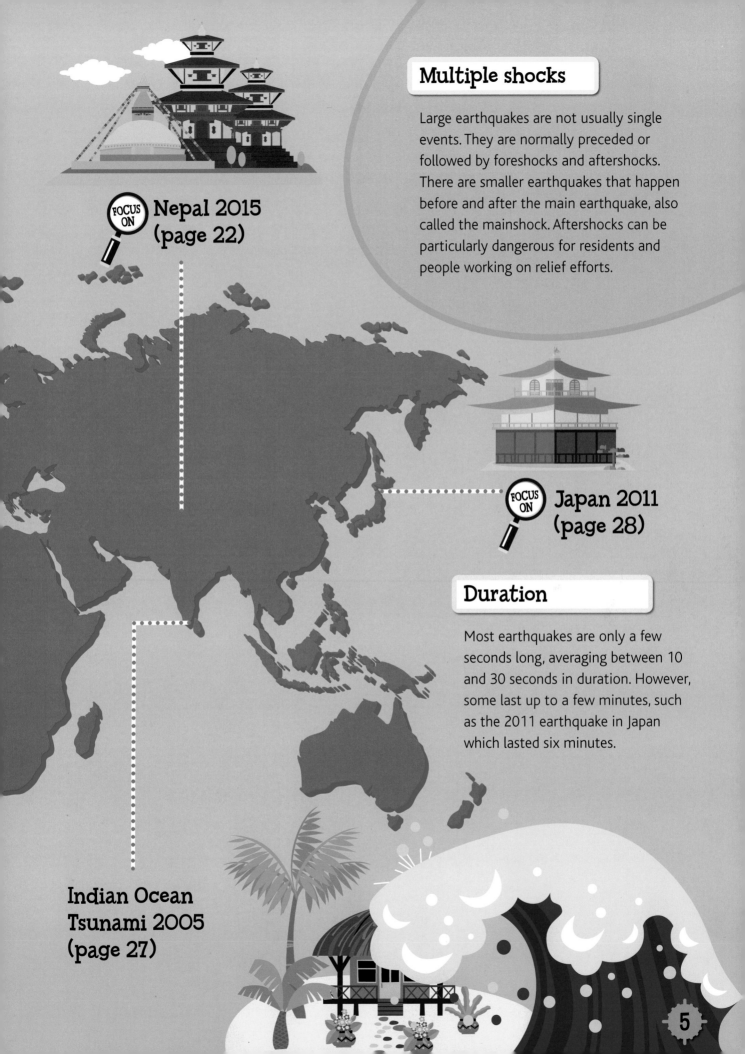

Multiple shocks

Large earthquakes are not usually single events. They are normally preceded or followed by foreshocks and aftershocks. There are smaller earthquakes that happen before and after the main earthquake, also called the mainshock. Aftershocks can be particularly dangerous for residents and people working on relief efforts.

Duration

Most earthquakes are only a few seconds long, averaging between 10 and 30 seconds in duration. However, some last up to a few minutes, such as the 2011 earthquake in Japan which lasted six minutes.

Tectonic Plates

If you could cut the Earth in half down the middle, you would see that it is not the same all the way through. Like an onion, the Earth has layers, and the outer layer, called the crust, is broken up into jigsaw-like pieces called tectonic plates. These tectonic plates are constantly moving, and it is this movement that causes earthquakes.

Compostition of the Earth

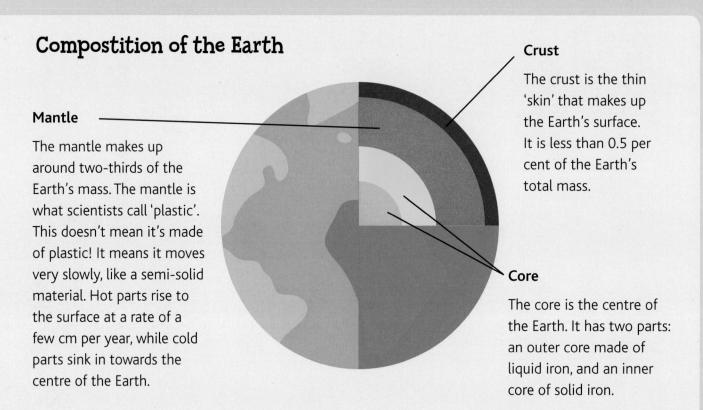

Mantle

The mantle makes up around two-thirds of the Earth's mass. The mantle is what scientists call 'plastic'. This doesn't mean it's made of plastic! It means it moves very slowly, like a semi-solid material. Hot parts rise to the surface at a rate of a few cm per year, while cold parts sink in towards the centre of the Earth.

Crust

The crust is the thin 'skin' that makes up the Earth's surface. It is less than 0.5 per cent of the Earth's total mass.

Core

The core is the centre of the Earth. It has two parts: an outer core made of liquid iron, and an inner core of solid iron.

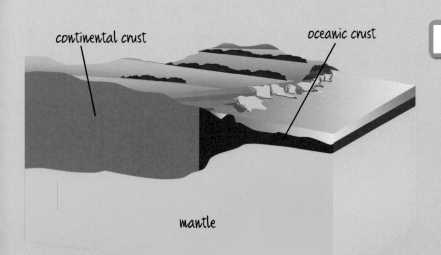

continental crust

oceanic crust

mantle

Types of crust

There are two different kinds of crust: oceanic and continental. Continental crust is the name given to the parts of the crust that make up the land. It is between 25 and 90 km thick, and made of lots of different types of rock. Oceanic crust is the part of the Earth's crust that makes up the ocean floor. It is thinner, at only 6 to 11 km thick. It is made mainly of basalt rock.

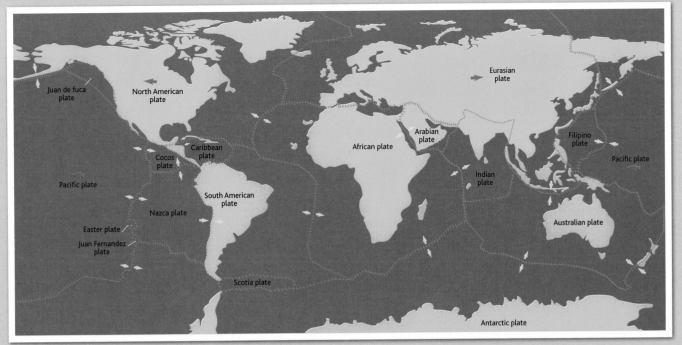

This map shows the edges of the tectonic plates. The arrows show the direction the plates are moving in.

Tectonic plates

The crust is broken up into tectonic plates. These large rocky slabs are joined to the mantle, and it is the movement in the 'plastic' mantle that causes the tectonic plates to move around on the surface at a rate of a few cm per year.

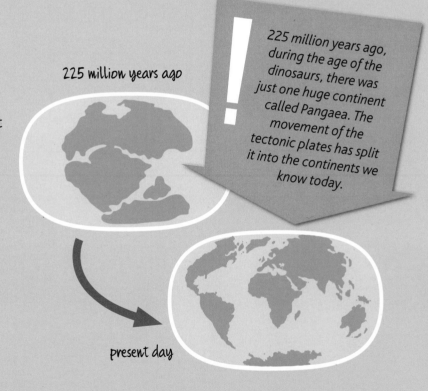

225 million years ago

present day

225 million years ago, during the age of the dinosaurs, there was just one huge continent called Pangaea. The movement of the tectonic plates has split it into the continents we know today.

Discovering the plates

In the 1960s, the USA tried to keep track of Russia's nuclear weapons testing by placing seismographs (which measure tiny vibrations in the ground) in 120 different places around the world. It was the data provided by these seismographs that revealed to scientists where earthquakes commonly occurred around the world. From this information, they were able to map the boundaries of Earth's tectonic plates.

Plate Boundaries and Faults

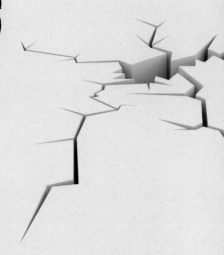

The place where two tectonic plates meet is called a plate boundary. Most earthquakes happen along plate boundaries. There are different types of plate boundary, depending on whether the two plates are moving apart, moving together or slipping alongside one another.

Destructive boundaries

Where two plates are moving together, this is called a destructive plate boundary. The effect of two plates meeting depends on whether they are both continental or oceanic plates, or a mix of both.

Subduction

When an oceanic plate meets a continental plate, the denser oceanic plate will slide underneath the continental plate. This is called 'subducting', and the area where one plate is sinking under another is called the subduction zone. The plates do not slide in an even motion, but a series of jerks, which cause earthquakes.

When two continental plates meet, they crumple upwards into mountain ranges. This is how the Himalayas were formed.

Constructive boundaries

Most constructive boundaries are under the ocean, between oceanic plates. As they move apart, the pressure on the mantle below is reduced, causing it to melt and rise upwards. It flows into the gap where it cools and solidifies, forming new crust.

Conservative boundaries

In some places, the two plates are not moving together or apart, but are sliding against one another. These are called conservative plate boundaries. As the plates try and grind past each other, strain builds up, which gets released as an earthquake.

Faults

All plate boundaries can also be called faults, which is a name geologists give to cracks in the Earth's crust. However, not all faults are plate boundaries. There are some cracks in the crust in the middle of tectonic plates, and earthquakes happen along these faults, too.

The whole length of a fault or plate boundary does not move at once during an earthquake. Instead, one part will slip and stick again, and other parts will not move, building up strain in areas near to recent quakes.

Pärvie fault

Lapland in Northern Sweden is nowhere near a plate boundary, but it is the location of the 155-kilometre Pärvie fault. During an earthquake 8000 years ago, the rock on one side of the fault rose up. This was due to the land expanding after the ice age. Previously the rock had been weighed down by incredibly heavy glacial ice. After the ice melted, the rock expanded upwards, causing a strong earthquake.

San Francisco 1906

In 1906, San Francisco was the largest city in the American West. It was a boom town, rich from gold mining, but residents of the bustling young city had no idea that they were sitting on the San Andreas Fault: part of the most active earthquake zone in the world.

FACT FILE

- 7.8 on the Richter Scale
- 60 seconds approximate duration
- 28,000 buildings destroyed
- 3,000 estimated killed
- 225,000 left homeless

Disaster

Early in the morning of the 18th April 1906, one of the worst natural disasters in US history occurred. An earthquake cracked the ground for about 480 km, almost half the length of California. The earthquake was one of the strongest ever; vibrations were felt from Coos Bay, Oregon, in the north, to Los Angeles in the south.

Coos Bay

San Francisco

Fault line

Los Angeles

USA

San Andreas Fault

The San Andreas Fault is the tectonic boundary between the North American Plate and the Pacific Plate. It is a conservative plate boundary. The Pacific Plate is moving in a northwest direction, and the North American Plate is moving in a relatively southwest direction. It slips an average of 33 to 37 mm per year.

Part of the San Andreas Fault in the Carrizo Plain National Park, visible from the air

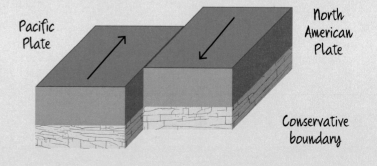

Pacific Plate

North American Plate

Conservative boundary

Fire

Many people were killed by falling debris and collapsing buildings. There were also many additional casualties during the aftermath of the quake. Electrical wires were torn, showering sparks onto the wooden-framed houses. Fires burned out of control across the city for three days and nights.

San Francisco was quickly rebuilt after the earthquake. Ideas were proposed for reorganising the layout of the city, but in the end many of the buildings were rebuilt in the same styles and locations as before.

The burnt City Hall building

Scientific breakthrough

In 1906, scientists did not understand much about how and why earthquakes happened. However, following the San Francisco earthquake, several US scientists studied how the ground had shifted throughout the area. They observed that in places, fences had been moved out of line. Through observing this pattern, scientists connected that the earthquake must be something to do with the nearby San Andreas Fault.

11

Measuring Earthquakes

The study of earthquakes is called seismology, and the scientists who study earthquakes are called seismologists. They measure the strength, locations and patterns of earthquake events.

Focus

The location of an earthquake can be described in two different ways. The first is called the focus. This is the actual point under the ground where the break in the rock first gives way, and it is the site of the greatest energy release. Seismic waves radiate from the focus in all directions. The closer to the surface the focus is, the more damage the quake can cause.

Epicentre

The other term for the location of an earthquake is the epicentre. The epicentre is the place on the Earth's surface directly above the focus.

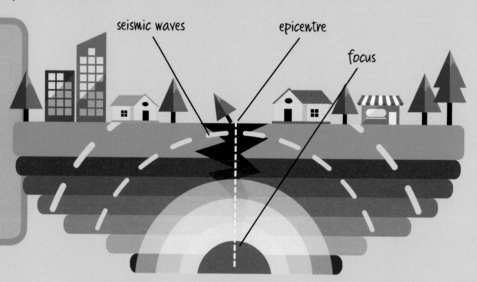

seismic waves   epicentre   focus

Seismic waves

The shockwaves that radiate out from an earthquake are called seismic waves, and there are several different types. Some travel through the ground, while others only travel at the surface.

P waves and S waves move inside the ground. Love waves and Rayleigh waves (named after the scientists who discovered them) only travel along the surface, and do the most damage to buildings.

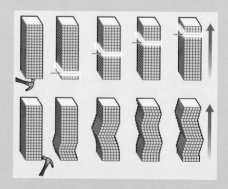

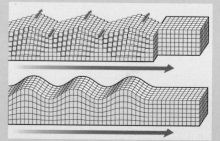

P waves are the first to be felt. They push and pull the ground back and forth.

S waves arrive next, and they move the ground from side to side.

Love waves move the ground from side to side, but only along the surface.

Rayleigh waves move along the surface in a wave motion.

Seismographs

The instruments that measure different seismic waves are called seismographs. By comparing how quickly the different types of wave arrive at the monitoring stations, scientists can pinpoint the location of the focus and epicentre of an earthquake.

In the past seismographs consisted of pendulums that recorded vibrations on paper. Modern seismographs use electromagnets and send the results straight to a computer for analysis.

Richter and Mercalli scales

Whenever you hear about an earthquake on the news, one of the key pieces of information is how big and strong it was. This is usually measured by the Richter Scale, however there is an alternative scale called the Mercalli Scale that is also sometimes used.

Richter Scale This measures the energy released by an earthquake by measuring the seismic waves.	Mercalli Scale This is based on how intense the earthquake feels to people, and how much damage is caused.	Approximate intensity at each level (damage caused depends on how deep or shallow the focus is).
1 - 2.9	I - III	Small, barely noticeable vibrations.
3 - 3.9	III - IV	Felt noticably. Objects might rock, heavy vibrations.
4 - 4.9	IV - V	Sleeping people awakened, some windows break.
5 - 5.9	V - VII	Minor damage to strong buildings, walls crack, chimneys fall in weak buildings.
6 - 6.9	VII - IX	Buildings heavily damaged, many collapsed.
7+	X - XII	Total destruction. Electricity, water and telephones cut off.

Earthquake Hazards

The most obvious hazard of an earthquake is the strong vibrations which can cause buildings to collapse. But several other hazards come from the environmental side-effects of the shockwaves, such as landslides and soil liquefaction.

Surface upheaval

One of the most recognisable effects of an earthquake is the cracking and tearing of the ground, as the seismic waves tear rocks apart along lines of weakness. Faulting is the term for when big blocks of rock move position in relation to one another during an earthquake. Surface upheaval can destroy infrastructure such as roads and bridges.

Landslides

The rock and soil that makes up hillsides and mountain slopes can be destabilised during an earthquake, causing large amounts of rock and debris to slip. Landslides can have devastating effects on settlements in their paths. A secondary effect of landslides can be that river channels become blocked, causing flooding.

Mudslides

Mud flows, or mudslides are a particular type of landslide where the soil is waterlogged. Being very fluid, they can travel farther and over shallower slopes than rocky landslides.

Avalanches

In snowy, mountainous regions, avalanches can be a dangerous secondary effect of earthquakes. Avalanches happen when large amounts of snow and ice become unstable and slide down a mountainside. Large avalanches can destroy or bury buildings in their path, and people can become buried in the snow.

Liquefaction

One strange effect that earthquakes can have is liquefaction. When soils and underground rocks contain water, the shaking caused by an earthquake can cause apparently solid ground to become quicksand. Buildings can sink straight into the ground. Foundations become undermined, breaking up roads and pavements.

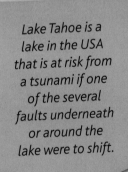

! Lake Tahoe is a lake in the USA that is at risk from a tsunami if one of the several faults underneath or around the lake were to shift.

The ground beneath this tarmac road has become liquefied.

Tsunamis

Earthquakes in the ocean can cause huge waves (read about ocean tsunamis on page 26), but even inland earthquakes can have some surprising effects. Earthquakes can cause rivers to flow backwards in 'fluvial tsunamis', and earthquakes can generate huge waves in inland lakes, posing a danger to settlements on lake shores.

Peru 1970

On 31 May 1970, a huge earthquake occurred off the coast of Peru. The shockwaves from the earthquake caused huge amounts of damage in coastal towns, but many fatalities were caused by secondary effects of the quake, including huge landslides.

FACT FILE

- 7.9 on the Richter Scale
- 45 seconds approximate duration
- 83,000 square km affected
- 70,000 estimated killed
- 800,000 left homeless

Destructive boundary

The earthquake occurred on the destructive plate boundary between the Nazca Plate and the South American Plate. The oceanic Nazca Plate is being subducted under the South American Plate, a tectonic movement which has also created the huge Andes mountain range over millions of years.

Coastal quake

The huge earthquake occurred under the Pacific Ocean, 25 km west of the coastal town of Chimbote. It struck at 3.23 pm in the afternoon, while many people were watching the Italy vs. Brazil FIFA World Cup match. Houses, bridges and roads collapsed across an area nearly the size of Portugal.

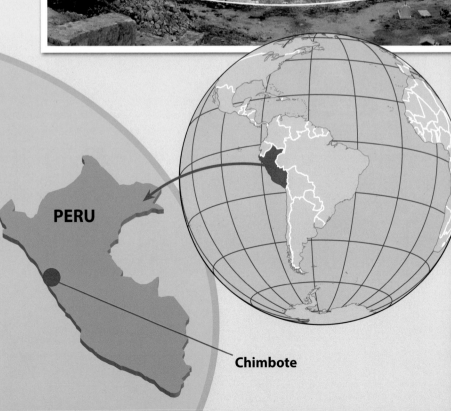

PERU

Chimbote

Fatal landslide

Due to the destabilising effect of the quake, a large part of the Huascarán mountain, Peru's highest peak, broke loose. This created a devastating landslide. Ten million cubic metres of rock and ice sped down the side of the mountain at 200 km per hour. As it slid, it accumulated another seventy million cubic metres of ice.

The light shaded area in this photo shows the area that was covered by the landslide.

Buried

The town of Yungay was directly in the landslide's path. Almost all of the town's 25,000 inhabitants were buried underneath the mud and boulders. The area covered by the landslide was afterwards declared a national cemetery, and a monument was built to remember the victims.

Due to the amount of ice and snow included in the landslide, it is also considered to be the deadliest avalanche in the world.

Earthquakes and Buildings

The main danger to people during earthquakes that happen in or near towns and cities is being killed or injured by falling buildings. However, some buildings can withstand much greater seismic forces than others.

Collapsing buildings

Buildings are placed under huge strain during an earthquake, as the ground is moving violently up and down, and from side to side. It is the side-to-side motion that is most damaging, as waves of energy travel up the walls cracking the entire building's structure and causing it to collapse.

Infrastructure damage

As well as buildings, bridges, roads, railways and utilities such as gas and water mains can be severely damaged. This can prevent people from being able to communicate or travel during the aftermath.

Fire

Burning buildings are a significant hazard. These can be caused by broken gas and electricity mains, as well as cooking fires used in developing countries.

Stronger buildings

Buildings can be engineered to better withstand earthquakes. The simplest way to improve buildings' chances of survival in a quake is simply to make them stronger: for example by adding extra steel to reinforce concrete walls to stop them crumbling.

Base isolation

Another way to improve a building's chance of survival is to cushion or isolate the foundations from the ground so as to reduce the amount of shaking that travels up the building. Techniques include building on flexible rubber bearings or pads. These work in a similar way to a bicycle's suspension that absorbs any jolting forces when travelling over rough ground.

Sideways forces

Buildings can have some flexibility built into them, with systems of shock-absorbing dampers that can compress and stretch during an earthquake to absorb the sideways motion.

!

The Torre Mayor is one of the most earthquake proof buildings in the world, able to withstand an earthquake of a magnitude of 8.5.

Torre Mayor

In 1985, Mexico City was the site of a devastating earthquake. One area of the city in particular suffered extreme damage due to soil liquefaction. Yet this was the site chosen to build a huge skyscraper, the Torre Mayor, in 2003. The Torre Mayor incorporated various anti-earthquake measures in its construction, including 90 huge diamond-shaped shock-absorbing dampers.

Rescue and Relief

Immediately after an earthquake, work begins on rescuing people who are trapped under collapsed buildings, and treating people who have been injured during the quake.

Where to look

Time is of the essence when it comes to rescuing trapped people, so rescue workers need to know where they are most likely to find survivors. They can ask local people for insight into where people may have taken shelter.

Stairwells

Spaces such as stairwells are often the strongest part of a building, where there are gaps that rescue workers call 'voids'. Survivors may be found having taken shelter in these spaces.

Sniffer dogs are often used as they are extremely good at locating survivors.

Technology

Survivors can be detected by using infra-red cameras fed through small cracks to locate people though their body heat. Specialist sound equipment can also be used to listen for people banging to get attention, and carbon dioxide monitors can sometimes locate people who are unconscious by measuring the CO_2 from their breathing.

Dangerous job

The work of excavating collapsed buildings to look for survivors can be extremely dangerous for the rescue workers themselves, as there is a risk that weakened buildings will collapse on them. Aftershocks also pose a large danger to people working during the aftermath of an earthquake.

Search and rescue attempts are usually called off between five and seven days after a disaster.

Blocked infrastructure

Damage to roads and communication systems can pose big problems for rescue and relief efforts, as hospitals might be made inaccessible when roads are destroyed, and information about where rescue teams are most needed cannot be communicated when telephone lines are down.

Food and housing

After the immediate aftermath, the challenges facing governments and relief agencies are feeding and housing people. Temporary shelters and tent cities might be erected to house people while earthquake clean up and rebuilding work is going on. Food and medical supplies may need to be transported by air while roads are blocked.

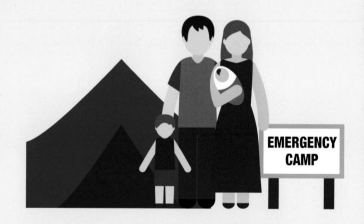

EMERGENCY CAMP

Disease

A further complication that earthquakes can cause is the spread of disease. Sewage systems and water treatment facilities can be disrupted, causing contamination of water supplies. Combined with people living in close quarters in temporary housing, and with poor medical attention, contagious diseases can spread very quickly.

Nepal 2015

Nepal is a country in the Himalayan region; an area of the world with a lot of seismic activity and rapid plate movement that has created the huge Himalayan mountain range over the last 40-50 million years. On 25 April 2015, a massive earthquake hit, affecting 30 of the country's 75 districts.

FACT FILE

- 7.8 on the Richter Scale
- 7.3 Richter aftershock on 12 May
- 77 km northwest of capital Kathmandu
- 9,000 killed
- 850,000 homes, schools and other buildings destroyed
- 80 years since the last major quake

Shallow quake

The epicentre of the earthquake was in Gorkha district, close to the country's capital city, Kathmandu. What made the quake particularly devastating was how shallow it was, with the focus being only between 11-15 km underground.

Plate boundary

The earthquake was caused by a sudden release of built-up stress between the Eurasian Plate and the Indian Plate that are colliding together at a rate of around 45 mm per year.

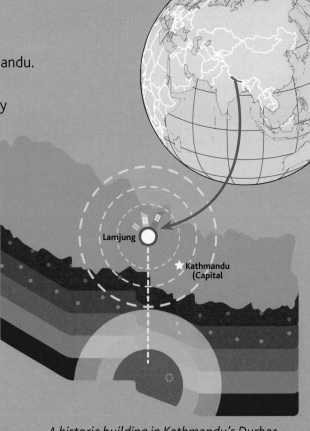

A historic building in Kathmandu's Durbar Square before and after the earthquake.

Monuments

Many temples and historical sites and monuments were destroyed in the quake. The Nepalese government plans to rebuild important monuments in the future.

Accessing victims

As Nepal is such a mountainous country, one of the key difficulties in the aftermath was reaching earthquake victims spread out in isolated villages. Many of the roads were blocked, and the only way to bring urgently needed medical help and aid, such as food and blankets, to the rural inhabitants was via helicopter.

Over
4.1 billion
US dollars was pledged in aid money from countries around the world to help with relief and reconstruction.

Aftershocks

Another huge problem for the rescue and relief efforts were the large number of powerful aftershocks. There were several hundred aftershocks of various sizes, including a huge 7.3 on the Richter Scale on 12 May, over two weeks after the original quake. These further destabilised damaged buildings and meant airports had to be closed, preventing essential aid from reaching the country.

! The earthquake caused deadly avalanches on Mount Everest, and a number of climbers and Sherpas (local Nepalese mountain guides) were killed.

Preparing for Earthquakes

Earthquakes are a fact of life for many people around the world. As of yet, we cannot predict exactly when an earthquake will occur, so preparing for earthquakes is an important part of minimising casualties and destruction when they do occur.

! Major cities such as San Francisco, Tokyo and Istanbul are at risk from earthquakes sometime in the next few decades.

• San Francisco

Earthquake forecasting

We know where the active faults are in the world, and seismologists are getting quite accurate about where along a fault an earthquake is likely to happen next. They do this by observing where past earthquakes have occurred and using this information to understand where stress is building up along the fault line. However, we are not yet able to give accurate predictions as to when exactly the predicted quakes will occur.

Ground movement

Scientists monitor the ground for movement to try and improve their understanding of the build-up of strain along faults. In California, laser beams are aimed across fault lines. If the time it takes for the beam to reach a reflector changes, scientists know the ground has moved.

Warning signs

There are examples of short notice warning signs and strange phenomena just before earthquakes that people have noticed in the past. These include animals behaving oddly, such as toads leaving their pools in large numbers, water levels changing in wells, and even a strange glow appearing in the sky.

DROP!

COVER

HOLD ON!

Earthquake drills

Knowing how to behave in an earthquake is important for residents of earthquake-prone areas. In earthquake-prone areas around the world, school children regularly practise earthquake drills. They must *Drop* to the floor, take *Cover* under a desk or similar, and *Hold* on until the quake ends.

• Istanbul

• Tokyo

In Japan, 1 September is 'Disaster Prevention Day' when all around the country people practise earthquake drills.

stick ornaments to shelves

attach furniture to wall

don't hang pictures over beds

Preparing your home

Shaking from earthquakes can cause damage and injury from unsecured objects inside the home. Precautions can be taken such as not hanging pictures with glass fronts over beds, bolting heavy furniture to the wall and fixing ornaments to shelves with putty.

Tsunamis

Many of the Earth's plate boundaries and faults lie on the ocean floor. Although earthquakes that occur on these boundaries might be thousands of miles from the nearest human settlement, they can still cause devastation due to a secondary hazard: tsunamis.

FACT FILE

- 1,000 kmph: the speed that a tsunami wave can travel across the ocean
- 30 cm: the possible height of a tsunami wave in the open ocean
- 35+ metres: the height a tsunami wave can reach once it gets to shore. That's taller than a ten storey building!

Fault movement

When a fault suddenly thrusts upwards or downwards underneath the ocean, the water above it is displaced. This causes a wave to radiate out across the ocean. In the middle of the ocean, the wave will be very small, but as it gets closer to shore and the sea bed gets shallower, the wave gains height.

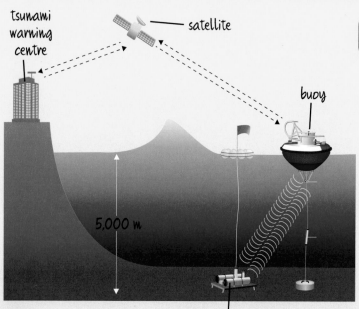

tsunami warning centre

satellite

buoy

5,000 m

water pressure sensor

Tsunami warning system

There are systems in place in certain locations, such as in the Pacific Ocean, to detect seismic activity, and convey the risk of a potential tsunami to the public in coastal areas. Buoys and sea level gauges out in the ocean can detect earthquakes and abnormal waves, and send the information via satellite to land. However, because tsunami waves can travel so fast, a warning system is not always effective if the earthquake occurs close to shore.

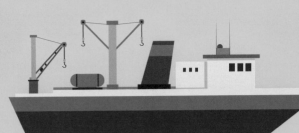

At sea, tsunami waves are small, so people on boats do not notice them.

The word 'tsunami' comes from the Japanese for 'harbour wave'. Fishermen at sea would not notice the tsunami wave pass when they were out fishing, but on returning to harbour they would see the destruction caused by a huge wave.

Pacific ocean

Most tsunamis occur in the Pacific Ocean, around the so-called 'Ring of Fire'. This is a ring of active subduction zones around the edge of the Pacific Ocean, where many earthquakes and volcanoes occur.

Pacific Ocean

Indian Ocean

The pink line here shows the 'Ring of Fire', the area around the Pacific Ocean where earthquakes and volcanoes are especially common.

Indian Ocean Tsunami

On Boxing Day 2004, there was a huge 9.0 magnitude earthquake on the floor of the Indian Ocean, which triggered a vast tsunami wave. It affected the shores of Indonesia, Sri Lanka, India, Thailand, Malaysia and even the east coast of Africa. There were no tsunami warning systems in place. 226,000 people died and 5 million were left homeless.

Devastation caused by the Boxing Day Tsunami in the Indian Ocean, 2004.

FOCUS ON Japan 2011

Located on the Pacific 'Ring of Fire', Japan is used to earthquakes. But no amount of drills and warning systems could avoid the damage wrought by the huge 9.0 magnitude earthquake off shore in 2011, and the tsunami that followed.

Sendai

epicentre

Japan

Record breaker

There were foreshocks for several days before 11 March 2011, when at 2.46 pm, a gigantic earthquake struck off the coast of Japan. It was particularly shallow, at a depth of only 32 km. It was the largest quake Japan had ever experienced, and the fifth largest ever recorded worldwide.

Tsunami

The real damage was caused not by the quake itself, but by the subsequent tsunami. The waves that hit the coast were so large that they picked up ships, cars and houses, and travelled 10 km inland. In places, the waves were 6 m high, and an area of 561 square km was flooded.

Nuclear catastrophe

The Fukushima nuclear plant on the coast of northeast Japan was hit by the tsunami wave, and the back-up generators designed to keep the plant from going into meltdown were destroyed. This caused several explosions in the plant, and radioactive material leaking into the surrounding area meant a 30 km radius had to be evacuated. Experts believe the clean up from the nuclear disaster could take up to 80 years.

Towns and villages were destroyed, creating millions of tons of rubbish.

Debris

Authorities in Japan estimated that there was a huge 25 million tons of debris caused by the quake and tsunami, making the clean-up operation a gigantic task. Clean-up was further complicated by needing to ensure rubbish that might be contaminated with radioactivity was not taken to other areas.

Glossary

aftershock a smaller earthquake after the main earthquake

avalanche a large movement of snow and ice downhill

base isolation rubber pads that a house is built on to absorb vibrations

conservative boundary a plate boundary where the two plates slide next to one another

aonstructive boundary a plate boundary where the two plates are moving apart

aontinental crust the type of crust that makes up the Earth's continental landmasses

aore the centre layer of the Earth

arust the thin rocky 'skin' layer on the surface of the Earth

destructive boundary a plate boundary where the two plates are moving together

drill method of practising how to behave during a distaster to stay safe

epicentre the place on the Earth's surface directly above the focus point of an earthquake

fault a large crack in the Earth's crust

fluvial tsunami when the flow of a river is reversed due to sudden ground movement

focus the point underground where an earthquake happens and shockwaves radiate out from

foreshock t smaller earthquake before the main earthquake

liquefaction when the ground acts like a fluid during an earthquake causing buildings to sink

mainshock the main release of seismic waves during an earthquake event

mantle the layer of the Earth under the crust that moves very slowly over time

Mercalli scale a scale that grades earthquakes according to how much damage they cause

oceanic crust the type of crust that makes up the ocean floor

Richter scale a scale that grades earthquakes according to how much energy they release

seismic waves the shock waves that are sent out by an earthquake, shaking the ground

seismographs sensitive machines that measure seismic waves

seismologist a scientist who studies earthquakes and their effects

seismology the study of earthquakes

subduction zone the area where one tectonic plate is being forced underneath another

surface upheaval the cracking and tearing of the ground due to an earthquake

tectonic plate one of the vast rocky slabs that make up the Earth's crust like a jigsaw

Test yourself!

1 What is the average duration of an earthquake?

2 Which of the two types of the Earth's crust is thinner and made mainly of the rock basalt?

3 Which of the following statements is correct?

a) All plate boundaries can also be described as faults.

b) All faults can also be described as plate boundaries.

4 What is the name of the fault that San Francisco sits on?

5 Is the epicentre of an earthquake on the surface of the Earth or underground?

6 What was the main cause of loss of life in the Peru 1970 earthquake?

7 What are the three actions carried out during an earthquake drill?

8 How fast can a tsunami wave travel across the ocean?

Check your answers on page 32.

Further reading

Nature Unleashed: Earthquakes
Louise and Richard Spilsbury (Franklin Watts, 2017)

Catastrophe: Earthquake Distasters
John Hawkins (Franklin Watts, 2014)

Websites

Read more about earthquakes at the following websites:

earthquake.usgs.gov/learn/kids

www.bgs.ac.uk/discoveringGeology/hazards/earthquakes

news.bbc.co.uk/cbbcnews/hi/find_out/guides/tech/earthquakes/news-id_1894000/1894934.stm

Index

Answers

1 10–30 seconds

2 Oceanic crust

3 a) is correct. Some faults are not plate boundaries, but cracks in the middle of a tectonic plate.

4 The San Andreas Fault

5 The epicentre is on the surface of the Earth. The focus is underground.

6 A huge landslide

7 *Drop* to the ground, take *Cover* underneath a table, *Hold* on until the shaking stops.

8 Up to 1,000 km per hour

GEOGRAPHICS
Series contents lists

Biomes
- What is a Biome? • Forests
- Yosemite • Rainforests • The Amazon Rainforest • Grasslands and Savannahs • The Serengeti
- Deserts • The Sahara Desert
- Tundra and Ice • Antarctica
- Oceans • The Great Barrier Reef
- Rivers and Lakes • The Nile River

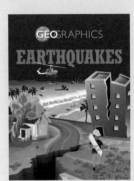

Earthquakes
- What is an Earthquake?
- Tectonic Plates • The San Andreas Fault • Creating Earthquakes
- Types of Earthquake • Shock Waves • Measuring Earthquakes
- The Lisbon Earthquake
- Tsunamis • The 2004 Tsunami
- Predicting Earthquakes
- Living with Earthquakes • Japan

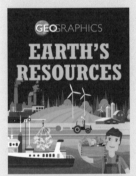

Earth's Resources
- What are Resources? • Mining
- Wood • Plastic • Recycling and Rubbish • Agriculture • GM Crops
- Fishing • North Sea Fishing
- Recycling • Fossil Fuels
- Sustainable Energy • Eco-cities

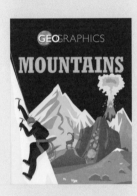

Mountains
- What is a Mountain?
- Moving Plates • Fold and Block Mountains • Volcanic Mountains
- The Andes • Changing Mountains
- The Alps • Climate • Biomes
- The Rocky Mountains • People and Mountains • The Himalayas
- Mountain Resources
- The Appalachian Mountains

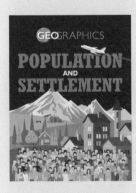

Population and Settlement
- What are Population and Settlement? • Distribution and Density • Population Growth
- Overpopulation • Population Structure • Uganda and Japan
- Migration • UK Migration
- Settlement Sites • Athens
- Settlement Layout • Manila
- Changing Settlements

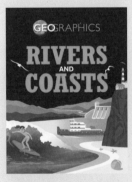

Rivers and Coasts
- Rivers and Coasts • River Structure • The Ganges River
- River Erosion • River Formations
- The Colorado River • Types of Coasts • The UK Coast • Changing Coasts • Arches and Stacks • The Twelve Apostles • People and Water • The Three Gorges Dam
- Flooding • Venice

Volcanoes
- What are Volcanoes?
- Formation • The Ring of Fire
- Stratovolcanoes • Mount Fuji
- Shield Volcanoes • Mauna Kea
- Calderas and Cinder Cones
- Eruption • Mount Vesuvius
- Lava • Underwater Volcanoes
- Dormant and Extinct Volcanoes

The Water Cycle
- What is the Water Cycle?
- Our Blue Planet • Evaporation
- Transpiration • Condensation
- Clouds • Precipitation • Rainfall
- Rain in the Himalayas
- Accumulation • River Basins
- The Mississippi River
- Water Stores • Polar Ice Caps
- Humans and the Water Cycle